REBIRTH
as Empirical Basis for
The Buddha's
Four Noble Truths

Suwanda H.J. Sugunasiri, PhD

SUMERU

REBIRTH
as Empirical Basis for
The Buddha's Four Noble Truths

Suwanda H. J. Sugunasiri, PhD
Founder / Professor,
Nalanda College of Buddhist Studies, Toronto, Canada;
Trinity College, University of Toronto

Design by Karma Yönten Gyatso

Published by
The Sumeru Press Inc.
PO Box 2089, Richmond Hill, ON
Canada L4E 1A3

ISBN 978-1-896559-04-9 (1st print edition)

For more information about The Sumeru Press
visit us at *www.sumeru-books.com*

Contents

A Brief Note About Notes

The endnotes are for the curious. That's where you go if you find yourself asking, "Says who?" or "What's the Pali term?" or you're hoping for some additional information, an explanation and the like. But you miss nothing by not going there!

Introduction

Rebirth (Re-becoming) is different from Re-incarnation.[1]

I know that the idea of 'rebirth' makes you want to grit your teeth. A well-known western Buddhist thinks it "odd that a practice concerned with anguish and the ending of anguish should be obliged to adopt ancient Indian metaphysical theories." He goes on to say, "In accepting the idea of rebirth, the Buddha reflected the worldview of his time."[2]

This is surprising. The Buddha is known to 'go against the current.'[3] As an example, he did not go along with the then current view that the heart is the seat of consciousness, as in the Upanishads.[4]

But before getting into it, let me see if the rough ride given birth by rebirth was come by honestly. Ah yes… isn't it linked to that Indian caste system, that untouchability, keeping millions of people in great suffering, and as social outcastes? And all this by divine decree!

But this is reincarnation, in Hinduism (more accurately Brahminism) – 'the doctrine that the soul reappears after death in another, and bodily, form' (Webster's). It is thus sometimes translated as 'transmigration of the soul.' As you can see, reincarnation entails 'ensoulment'– having a 'soul' implanted by a Godhead.[5]

What I'm talking about is rebirth, again, as in Webster's – 'a new or second birth.' In fact, 're-becoming'[6], i.e., 'renewed existence' or 'new birth' as in the Pali Dictionary[7], captures the Buddhian[8] concept better.

And the Buddha teaches anattà 'asoulity' (my term)[9], i.e., the absence of any such thing as a soul. So there's no question of ensoulment. This is also because Buddha sees no place for a creator God[10] – Brahma in Vedism (Yahweh, Allah, etc. in others), in charge of the operation.

And, as to caste, here's what the Buddha has to say:

> Not by birth is one a Vasala;
>
> not by birth is one a Brahmin.
>
> But by deed alone …

By Vasala, of course, is meant an 'untouchable.'

So then let's be clear what I'm talking about. It is Buddha's Teaching of 'rebirth,' 're-becoming,' and NOT the Hindu concept of 're-incarnation'[11], although many a native-English writer seem to use them interchangeably. And, wrongly, I might add, as we shall see, creating confusion.

Buddha's Three Knowledges

With this distinction in mind, let's transport ourselves to that critical, historic night over 2500 years ago, when the Buddha came by[12], not one, but three 'Knowledges'[13]. We can come to the other two later, but let's first go to the third, the one that turned a wandering ascetic Samana Gotama into Gotama 'Buddha.' This, of course, was the discovery, or coming by the Knowledge, of the Four Noble Truths[14]:

1. 'suffering' (i.e., the reality of...),

2. 'arising,' (the cause of suffering),

3. 'cessation' (the ending of suffering) and

4. 'path' (the way to ending of suffering)[15].

(Can we come to the details later?)

Buddhist literature divides a night into three 'watches.' Let us note, then, that this third knowledge was gained in the Third Watch of the night (roughly 2 – 6 am). And, though it would be obvious, let us remember that the Third Watch comes after the First Watch (6 – 10 pm) and the Second Watch (10 pm – 2am). Of course, as in statistics, the boundaries are approximate.

The First Watch

Let us now return to the beginning – Knowledge I, in the First Watch. So what knowledge was it that he gained? It was 'the memory of living in past lives'[16]. It is 'knowledge' because it is something he hadn't known before. And so, it must've been like you watching a double movie, because he was at it for a full four hours (6 – 10 pm)! In other words, what the texts say is that the Samana ('wanderer') Gotama (remember, he is not yet the Buddha) literally saw how he himself was born in several life-times[17]. And here's the (later) Buddha making one such connection between this life and a previous life: "At that time, Ananda was the younger brother, but the elder was I myself"[18]. What Samana Gotama came by, then, in this First Watch, was this *empirical* confirmation of his own birth in several life-times. Empirical, to emphasize. To me, this is like Darwin[19] collecting some initial samples at the Galapagos Islands. Just individual bits and pieces of information.

But how on earth did the Samana Gotama come to see his past lives? He "initiated energy, undeterred, attained to self-possession, not distracted, calmed his body, not excited, and concentrated his thoughts, focused on one point"[20]. Let's remember that, after leaving the Palace, he – Prince Siddhartha, had gone to the two leading meditation maestros of the time, Alara Kalama and Uddaka Ramaputra. Under the last, he was able to reach a meditation state called 'the sphere of neither perception nor non-perception'[21] – far beyond any ordinary consciousness Psych 101 will teach you about.

But he now leaves the maestros. Meditating in seclusion in the bush all by himself, he would soon arrive at even a higher point of sharpness of mind called 'cessation of perception'[22]. Sure it was, on this historic day, still his own consciousness that he was looking at. But now, still, in his own words, focused on one point (see above), he was going deeper and deeper, when he, accidentally, we might say, stumbles upon the consciousness of his own past lives. Accidentally we say because he was not looking for it. In fact, he was not looking for anything; simply refining, honing in, the focus of his mind.

So the knowledge of his own past lives was come by honestly, through sheer perseverance and singlepointedness[23]. Or, 'needlepointedness,' if you like, capturing the idea better visually. So sharp was the focus! Sharper than a scientist looking at an atom, or a cell, under a microscope, wouldn't you say? The training of a scientist, as we know, does not include training in mind concentration.

So it was this personal verification, as in any good science, that provided the Buddha with the epistemological justification for it to be called 'knowledge,' or 'science'[24].

Let us note for the record here again that what we are talking about is a 'knowledge' that the Buddha came by, and not a 'belief' arrived at in hallucination, or in some airy-fairy ecstasy.

The Second Watch

Let's then continue to watch Samana Gotama. Shh!

Equipped with one empirical confirmation, he continues to maintain 'self-possession, not distracted, calm[ing] his body, not excited,' and still 'focused on one point.' He now begins to see, in the Second Watch (roughly 10 pm to 2 am), additional Rebirths. But now it is not of himself exclusively, but relating to many others, as if watching multiple movies! The mind comes to be inundated with the high drama of living – in joy and suffering, love and hate, conflict and resolution...

But which others? To wax poetic:

Was it the lives of every Dick, Jane, Deepa and Ming on earth?

Not by a country mile! 'Twas his own kith n' kin, at the hearth,

rubbin' in on 'im, in a bees' bumble,

in happy banter, or in a rough n' tumble!

So it was the lives of those with whom he had been interacting in his own past lives that he was now seeing. This would have been likely from the most recent to the furthest back. These were people and events he had seen, heard, felt, smelled, touched, touched by, tasted, experienced and thought about. To give it a technical aura, these were stimuli that had left an imprint on his consciousness[25]. Or foot-prints in the memory lane, over lifetimes.

Oh here, he is in one of his past lives. Ah, he's in love! And his focus immediately falls on that partner. What thoughts and behaviours brought them together, and what brought the partner and himself happiness and unhappiness? This then naturally leads him to significant others – parents (his own and the partner's), offspring, friends, enemies, neighbours, etc. And, of course, others whom he had encountered – saints, crooks, buffoons, the wise, artists and con-artists and all!

This, then, would be like Darwin collecting additional samples.

So we may say that what he saw were the past lives of his kith and kin, apparently traveling together, in clusters. This, interestingly, reminds us of a similar pattern as science would discover – that certain types of matter seem to cluster together[26]. Just as again such clusters of matter change partners and relationships, so do the human cluster members, we could say. Changing roles, today's partner an offspring, parent or combatant in another life, sage or villain in yet another, happy or miserable, underachiever/overachiever, etc., in other lives, other times. Samana Gotama would encounter people being born, falling sick, ageing and dying as well.

No, we don't want to be technical about all this, but we do take a commercial break here, with your permission, for an interesting excursion. The Pali word capturing the idea of being born again and again is samsara, popularly 'Life Cycle.' But the Dictionary gives its literal meaning as 'faring on'[27], fitting the bill as above. But we may also note with relevance that samsara, even more literally, means 'moving along together'[28].

Texts describe what Samana Gotama gained in this second Watch as 'knowledge of exiting (= dying) and being born'[29], "…according to their actions, bad conduct leading to misery and good conduct to a good destiny"[30].

So as we can see, Knowledge II, just as Knowledge I, also results from personal verification, empirically, i.e., after the fact. So, no belief here either. Empirical is the key term.

A word about 'empirical.' First I only mean to say that the Knowledge of past lives, and of the process of exit and re-being, was arrived at after the fact, *a posteriori* to go academic, and not *a priori*.

At the stage of Cessation of Perception (as above), which he is at, Samana Gotama indeed can be said to be with, to borrow from Locke, a *tabula rasa*, literally, "a blank slate upon which experience writes the entire script...."[31] We may remember that he had left Uddaka Ramaputra, after having reached the highest meditative state under his direction. But this was still a form of 'perception.' After leaving him, however, he comes to be in the sphere/plane of 'cessation of perception' (see above). This means there was now simply NO sensory input to his consciousness. Period.

In every living moment of your life, the Buddha explains, your consciousness is bombarded with stimuli. On the one hand, it is through the five senses – eye, ear, nose, tongue and body. And then through the sixth sense – the mind. Here, the consciousness (which is another name for mind) is impinged upon by the mind itself.[32] The stimuli, external and internal, impacting on the consciousness, results in perception. But now, at this final stage, no such perceptions are being formed, which is why it is called 'cessation of perception,' literally, a 'blank sheet.'

And so, it is an absolute *objectivity* that he had, then, brought to that First, and now, the Second Watch of the night. This objectivity can be said to be even better than that of a scientist who comes to an experiment with a hypothesis. We may remember that Samana Gotama was also not trying to prove anything, even to himself. He was engaged in what may be called 'pure observation,' an empiricism – 'Search for knowledge by observation and experiment', as Webster's puts it. Observation indeed is precisely what Samana Gotama did.

As for experiment , again ditto. That is what he was doing by leaving the two teachers – trying to see for himself how far he can go in meditation, and what it would bring.[33]

The Third Watch

Let us continue to watch Samana Gotama now, continuing on to the Third Watch (approximately 2 – 6 am). Shh! He's still steady in deep meditation, unperturbed by the sounds of nature – early birds, a startled deer, water nearby, while the hand of time keeps ticking away.

He had now been watching, in the first two watches, the drama of a chockfull of suffering at the theatre of life. For a full eight hours. By the end of Watch Two, seeing he himself, and his kith and kin, going through the hoops of multiple lives, we could now see him putting his hands on his head, symbolically speaking, of course – remember he's in meditation, and saying, "Oh man, what suffering!" And this is exactly what we have as the first of the Four Noble Truths (see endnote 15 if you like) – the single term *dukkha*. In fact, this could be seen as the quintessence summation of Samana Gotama's experience of the first two Watches.

That suffering is a reality of life – though undoubtedly lazed with happiness, joy, excitement, hope, despair, and a whole slew of emotions, was no longer a question mark for him. Yes, growing up, he may have seen disease, old age and death as life's experiences. But it was only on this critical night that he saw them in his mind's eye, i.e. personally, and had the occasion for critical self-reflection.

The Theory of Rebirth (*Re-becoming*)

In this last Watch, something else is going on as well in Samana Gotama's mind. In Watch One, we see him simply making mental notes of his different lives. In Watch Two, he continues to collect more data, now in relation to others. But in this very process, his refined and sharpened mind begins to go into an analytical mode. Now begins a process of synthesizing the data, with some hypotheses emerging. Seeing a pattern, rebirth as reality emerges – the fact of and the how of exit consciousness and relinking consciousness[34]. Should we indeed not call it the Theory of Rebirth?

By way of analogy, let's think Darwin again. As he continues with collecting samples, certain hypotheses about species life begin to emerge in his mind. And later, back in the lab, the Theory of Evolution jumps to his mind. In the case of Samana Gotama, of course, the lab was his own mind. It is thus that the Theory of Rebirth jumps into his mind[35].

So, to repeat once again, the Theory of Rebirth is based in empirical evidence. We call it a 'theory' since it is the outcome of a process of systematization going on in the mind based on the data collected over the night.

The First Noble Truth

Now this personal conviction of the reality of suffering, and the freshly minted Theory of Rebirth, move his mind to a still higher analytical gear. It captures succinctly the nature of suffering he had seen in relation to himself and others: separation from loved ones is suffering, union with unloved ones is suffering, but even more basically, that "Birth is suffering"[36].

That's not all. Now suffering comes to appear not as an isolated fact, but as the first leg of a theory. Thus emerges the First Noble Truth, namely, dukkha 'suffering'! Again empirically based, we may note.

We may also note how suffering was noted by Samana Gotama as being part of a system of just desserts over a birth-death-rebirth life cycle, of himself and of others. So we can only conclude that the First Truth is grounded in the Theory of Rebirth. In other words, without that experience of the First and the Second Watches, there would have been no First Noble Truth.

The Second Noble Truth

But how about the Second Truth? Still at the theatre of life, watching and reflecting on its ups and downs, in relation to himself and to others, a trace of another leg of the emerging system appears. And it is that suffering arises from thirsts[37] (also translated as 'craving,' 'attachment'). They are called thirsts, because they need to be quenched all the time, crossing the desert of life. It suggests itself as another leg because it is inherent to sentience – i.e., present in all sentient beings (i.e., both human and animal)[38].

In his observations of '… bad conduct leading to misery and good conduct to a good destiny,' Samana Gotama cannot but fail to note how his own suffering was caused in the ever-going attempt to quench the thirst of his senses – eye, ear, nose, tongue, body and mind. The mind, of course, is, in Buddhian thought, as noted, the sixth sense[39]. As the Buddha would put it later, "All beings are food-based[40]." But the food he refers to is not only what we eat and drink, but also what we feed our senses with. He should know. As a Prince, it was a life of indulgence he had lived. But now he was seeing how the senses have been fed in his own past lives, with other things. And so of others. Seeing a comparable basis for the suffering of self and others, another generalized hypothesis – of 'sense thirst,' now comes to suggest itself.

Reminds you of Eros, Freud's 'pleasure principle'[41]?

Another insight that comes to the emerging Buddha on the basis of the same data is that sense-thirst comes from what comes to be called the 'thirst to be.' Simple enough? Just as we keep feeding our senses because we want to, we feed them because we want to 'be' as well! The only way we can get the good life we thirst for so much is by continuing to live. Shall we put it this way: we need to be at the Ball to have a ball of a time! So this wanting to be at the ball, i.e., to be alive, is what then comes to be generalized as the 'thirst to be,' the second thirst that makes up the Second Truth.

So now you're at the Ball, and want to be there longer. But you're exhausted. All the dancing has killed your feet! Put another way, your energy cells have been on overdrive, for far too long. So you leave.

You're in a reflective mood the next morning, and the faint thought appears on the screen of your mind: Hey, didn't I have to leave the fun, before I could continue to have fun again?

This exactly is what emerges in Samana Gotama's Enlightenment-in-process mind now: 'thirst to be not.' He had seen his own past lives, and then in relation to others – how each life came to an end. So on the basis of this empirical observation emerges the 'thirst to be not,' i.e., the Thirst to die theory, if you like.

Does the Greek concept of Thanatos i.e., 'death-personified' (Webster's), come to mind[42]?

The next day (week, month, year), you are back at another Ball, with new energy cells. In another of your reflective moods, you realize that leaving the Ball was only the first step you had to take in order to have fun. You had to return to the Ball, too.

We now recall what Samana Gotama saw in the Second Watch – of people not only 'exiting' (i.e., dying) (read: leaving the Ball) but also 're-linking' (being born) (returning to the Ball).

In yet another reflective mood, you now begin to see the necessary connection between leaving the Ball and returning – that you can't have one without the other. Interestingly, this, as we have seen, was Buddha's very insight – that the thirst to be and the thirst to be not, life and death if you like, are twins – always going hand in hand. But more – that life and death are in a cycle. If you want to continue to quench your sense thirst, first you must have the thirst! To have thirst, one has to be born again! But to be born again, you have to first die …, etc., round and round the garden, like a Teddy Bear, as the children's song goes.

Now, to make another digression, if I may, isn't it interesting that science tells us the same thing? Take e.g., that first cell that comes to be formed at conception, making up a new life. In the next particle-second, as scientists call it, it divides itself into two. This is called mitosis. The 'one' has 'died,' if only in the process of giving birth to 'two.' By 'dying,' of course, is not meant that it totally disappears, with no trace left, but that certain changes take place, as for example in shape and size – 'mutation' is what science calls it. One small, infinitesimal amount of matter goes dysfunctional, which is what serves as the condition to form into two cells, etc. It is this going dysfunctional that constitutes 'death.' It is a 'death' since the first no longer exists exactly as it was 100 per cent, and has given way, generating a second existence after itself, but with the same structure – DNA, nucleus, cell wall, etc.

Likewise when the twosome cell divides itself into four, sixteen, thirty two, etc., until the cells come to be in the billions, as is the case with sentient beings (including the animal kingdom, of course). Here again, 'death' takes place at each division. The ear, e.g., is not just any old cells, but cells that have reoriented themselves, parts of it dying, adjusting in relation to the other cells, in order to allow for the ear to take shape. So, of course, with all the parts of our body – nose, toes, hair, brain, etc.

If what science tells us is about just 'living' and 'dying' (of cells), Buddha's insight was that before living and dying was 'being born.' And that, therefore, what life entails is a cycle of continuity. It is this, then, that can be said to have brought him the insight of Rebirth.

This continuity, of course, relates to a given, single, human being. But if we can think at the level of the human species, this cycle of death and rebirth may be seen as nothing but an evolutionary imperative – the 'continuity of species,' to put in Darwinian terms. It is an 'imperative,' because it is natural. For the species to continue, it must happen. Otherwise, there would be no evolution.

So now we see that thirst is not just twins but triplets – 'sense-thirst,' 'thirst to be' and 'thirst to be not'[43]. It is this triple source of thirst, then, that emerges as the Second Noble Truth – 'arising' (samudaya; see item 2, Endnote 15), as texts simply put it.

We have seen that this Second Truth, in terms of all three 'thirsts,' has also emerged as insights from the experience of each getting due dessert in succeeding lives, negative and positive. So we may say that the Second Noble Truth also comes to be a natural concomitant of Knowledges I and II, namely the Rebirth process (of the many lives of himself and others). Indeed we find the Buddha making the specific connection: "What indeed, brethren, is the arising of dukkha? That thirst that is connected with re-becoming"[44].

The Third Noble Truth

On to the Third Truth, called 'cessation.' Cessation of just what?

Prince Siddhartha's renunciation was nothing but a let go of a life of royal indulgence. What he mastered throughout the six years since then was letting go of even more of the vestiges of craving, attachment, greed, anger, animosity and the like, hiding in the nooks and crannies of the cave of the mind. And the more he shed them, the calmer and peaceful he felt. And clearer his mind – lesser ignorance, more wisdom.

Still in the thick of the experience of experiencing life, the obvious insight now leaps to his mind: it was the letting go that had brought him the calm, and happiness, and had ended his own suffering of his secular life. And now, it was letting go of even more, the subtler traces. Here then emerges the Third Truth.

Sense-thirst, with the thirsts to be and to be not in tow, is what keeps life going. These are the passengers in the train of life. Driving the train are passion, anger and ignorance[45].

Passion and anger are obvious enough – the ware of everyday living. But ignorance? Ignorance of what?

Ah! On the one hand, this is the voluntary ignorance of not wanting to even acknowledge that suffering exists. I'm OK, you're OK syndrome. Shall we say that this ignoring is nothing more than a lobster that keeps prancing in a pot of water over the fire until the water begins to get hot (to use the poetic rendering of a 15th

c. Sinhala poet-monk, Vidagama Maitreya[46]).

On the other hand, ignorance is not being able to convince oneself of the need to cut off the thirsts, and to ditch the 'driver' behind it.

So cessation, then, is of passion, anger and ignorance.

And oh, by the way, cessation also means no more birth. Declares the Buddha (later, upon Awakening): "This is my last birth;" "No more re-becoming now!"[47]. No more birth means, of course, no more death! Neat! Which is why Nibbana comes to be called 'the unborn'[48]. This 'freedom from birth' (as Texts put it) surely cannot be a reference to this life; you're already born! Nibbana also comes to be called 'deathless'[49]. Logical, isn't it? No birth, no death!

Here, then, emerges the Third Noble Truth. Jettison the driver – passion, anger and ignorance, purifying the mind. Driver ditched, there won't be a question of passengers (thirsts), or the train (= life-cycle of samsara). And that's a guarantee, Buddha tells us, foolproof and watertight!

Voila, in this Third Watch, then - and my best guesstimate would be between 3 and 4 in the morning, Samana Gotama experiences Nibbana, literally 'blowing out!' As texts put it, he was now 'one who had cut off the flows'[50], becoming an Arhant 'Worthy One' as well, when '[re]birth is destroyed'[51].

So the Third Noble Truth, too, is again grounded in the data of the first two Watches – Rebirth.

The Fourth Noble Truth

Now he, the Buddha become, has seen the reality of suffering, its causes and the ending of suffering. He has also ended his own suffering, his flows cut off. This means that he had personally achieved what he had set out to achieve, namely, to find out just what this 'nirvana' was[52]. This was a term and concept already making the rounds in the 'body spiritual' of his time (sorry, 'body politic' wouldn't wash here). So it would not be unfair to assume that what prompted him in his effort to find out the nature of reality would have been his compassion. Wouldn't the tenacity and the relentlessness of suffering he had just seen, and the helplessness of those in its grip, move a mountain? So it would only be natural that his compassion would also lead him to look for a way of helping the helpless. Buddha is, after all, the 'Great Compassionate One'[53], isn't he, with 'wisdom' in balance, of course, making him also the 'Wise One'?

So the thought likely came to him, "I've spent six years at this. But what about these other poor humans, including my kith and kin? How are they going to be able to make a beginning towards what I myself have achieved, even as they go about living their normal lives?" That's when the Fourth Noble Truth, namely the Path[54] can be said to have emerged – to guide others towards jettisoning the cankers.

And so, it becomes clear how the Fourth Noble Truth, too, is grounded in Knowledges I and II, bringing out the reality of Rebirth (and Kamma, though not discussed[55], but for the same reasons as above).

Becoming Buddha

We have seen how in the very process of knowing the Third Truth, Samana Gotama's own personal inner devils come to be vacuumed out, his mind coming to be purified of the cankers behind existence. But now, coming by the Fourth Truth, he also comes to see the four Truths as a System. So it is coming to know these Truths, both individually and collectively then, the Eureka, the aha moment (see Endnote 35), that turns a Samana Gotama to Buddha, 'the Knowing One,' 'the Awakened One'! My best guess is between 4 and 5 am, in the Third Watch[56].

A double helix[57] alright: two strands, one in the left brain (Buddhahood), the other in the right brain ('Nibbanahood'), both reaching the highest perfection (as understood in Buddhian terms), in relation to each other. This would be to come by Knowledge III, characterized as the 'Knowledge of eliminating the flows'[58]. And it is made up of the Four Noble Truths.

Knowledges Based in Re-Birth

We have seen, then, that the Four Noble Truths, making up Knowledge III, taken both separately and collectively, have been squarely grounded in the experience of Rebirth (and Kamma). So we now see that becoming Buddha itself is founded in the experience of Rebirth (see end of article for a Chart outlining this in detail).

To deny this empirical basis, and separate the experience of Rebirth/Kamma from the discovery of the Four Noble Truths, then, would be like saying that Darwin's Theory of Evolution emerged without the data collected at Galapagos! Or that Einstein's Theory of Relativity emerged without the study of energy and matter. If that is all far-fetched, how about your own experience in reading this – that you have come to understand me, or agree/disagree with me, without going over the material over the last few pages.

Further, deny Buddha the first two Knowledges – let's see now… Oh yes, the knowledge of former lives and the process of exiting and re-becoming, you take away the last, namely, the knowledge 'eliminating the flows'! And then we make the Four Noble Truths a belief, based in no experiential knowledge of reality, violating Buddha's own principle of not accepting anything without personal verification. And, all of a sudden, it becomes a guesswork, out of the blue, that just happened to make sense.

But certainly most ironically and disturbingly, if you reject Rebirth as mere mythology, then no one, Buddhist or other, would have a logical, empirical basis to accept the Four Noble Truths as reality. However, let's say that the Four Noble Truths are accepted on the basis of faith, or confidence, because "the Buddha teaches so." Then one would have absolutely no choice but to accept Rebirth, too, because he says so, too! Taken to its logical conclusion, to not accept Rebirth would be tantamount to declaring that the Buddha is after all not Buddha 'the Knowing One!' He is not 'the Awakened One' either, just one dreaming in technicolour!

It would also be to relegate Buddha's discovery of the Four Noble Truths to the realm of philosophical speculation, a 'metaphysical Theory' lamented by our Buddhist scholar (see note 2), and not a 'come and see' empiricism[59], making a philosopher out of an empiricist/'analyst'[60]. What this says is that the Buddha, then, was only philosophizing, meaning 'speculating'! And He didn't discover!

Finally, it also means to embrace a materialism – that there is only this one life, namely, annihilism, which the Buddha categorically refutes along with the other extreme, eternalism[61].

Same Data,
Different Interpretation

The two inter-related phenomena of Rebirth and Kamma were undoubtedly part of the Indian Brahminic culture. So to that extent the two concepts may be justifiably seen as a vestige of Indic culture. But the point is that that was NOT the basis upon which the Buddha teaches them as part of his understanding. It was on the basis of his own discovery, through personal experience. And so the difference lies in the differential interpretation of the same data by Indic culture (and Hinduism) and the Buddha[62].

So to relegate Buddha's theory of Rebirth to the dustbin of an 'ancient Indian metaphysical theory' would be to, pardon the mixed metaphor here, throw the baby out with the bathwater. In fact, it would as well be not dissimilar to rejecting Einstein's interpretation of the nature of matter and energy, mistaking it (without personally verifying, of course) with Newton's (wrong) interpretation of the same data!

Clearly, nothing that has been said above provides 'proof' for rebirth. My attempt was rather to establish the validity of the concept of Rebirth / Kamma from a canonically based Four Noble Truths perspective, taking the latter (kamma) as a given (i.e., not argued for). On that basis, then, for a last hurrah, let me assert that Rebirth is not a belief, except for the 'willing-blind' who would rather not look at the evidence.

Let us remind ourselves that NO Teaching of the Buddha has thus far been proven to be wrong in its 2500 year history[63]. That surely is a better record than science itself! The fact that science may yet to discover rebirth/rebecoming is not a license to say that a given teaching of his is wrong.

But if you're a scientist, or of a scientific bent, yet to be convinced of the reality of Rebirth, can I invite you to kindly do what scientists do. Simply try it out for yourself, just as you would regarding, say, Einstein's Theory of Relativity. Luckily, you don't have to be a scientist to test out Buddha's Theory of Rebirth. Just sit in meditation, long and disciplined enough. It's in fact, something any Dick, Jane, Deepa and Ming can do, with effort, mindfulness and a curiosity to know. 'Establishing of Mindfulness' (satipaṭṭhāna)[64] is the meditation specifically developed by the Buddha for this very purpose – of understanding reality[65].

Willing to take up the challenge? If you're not ready yet – and that's understandable, the respectable position would be to hold judgment, and say out loud, with a sense of humility, "I just don't know. I have no evidence to accept it, but I have done no personal exploration to reject it either." Thank you! You just made me feel good that you've returned to your inherent or acquired scientific objectivity, away from a non-scientific western materialism that recognizes not the cyclical nature of sentience while at the same time venerating the equally cyclical Theory of Relativity relating to matter. Talk about contradicting!

Timeline

Allow me to end this exposé on a personal note, if I may. As a Buddhist practitioner, having gone to the extent I've gone arguing for the reality of Rebirth, from a canonical point of view, let me say that it matters to me not one whit; you read me right, it matters to me not one whit, spiritually speaking that is, whether Rebirth (and Kamma) are reality or myth. Two lines from another medieval Sinhala poet, Alagiyawanna Mukaveti, come to mind:

Whether there be a future life, or there be not,

'Tis best away from the unskilled, the whole lot[66]!

Inspired by these lines, reflecting the Buddhian spirit, I'm happy to keep my watch on the present moment, which really is all I could have any control over in any case. The future will take care of itself. And to spend my time speculating whether Rebirth is reality or not would not be to spend my time wisely, or fruitfully. The Buddha tells a beautiful story. If you were to be shot by an arrow, what would you rather do? Wonder about from which direction it came, try to size up the shooter, etc. or rather attend to the wound immediately.

Reconstruction

A Canonically-based Intuitive Reconstruction of the Process of Samana Gotama becoming Buddha, through the Three Watches of the Night, attaining both Nibbana and Buddhahood

(Chart to be read from the bottom upwards)   © 2009, Suwanda H J Sugunasiri

WATCH	TIME PERIOD	KNOWLEDGE TYPE	WATCH DETAIL	CONTENT	DETAILED CONTENT	SPIRITUAL STATUS
3	6 AM ↑ 2 AM	III 'Knowledge of getting rid of flows' (*āsavakkhaya ñāṇa*) END OF (RE)BIRTH (*ajāta*); END OF DEATH (*amata*))	5 – 6 AM ↑	Path (*magga*) ↑	EXCELLENT SAMMĀ: Concentration *samādhi* Mindfulness *sati* Exercise *vāyāma* Livelihood *ājīva* Conduct *kammanta* Language *vācā* Conceptualization *samkappa* View *diṭṭhi*	Buddha theorizing on the Path ↕ in the Bliss of Emancipation
			4 – 5 AM	'Cessation' (*nirodha*)		Attaining Buddhahood ↕ Attaining Nibbana
			3 – 4 AM ↑ 2 – 3 AM	'Arising' (*samudaya*) ↑ 'Suffering' (*dukkha*) ↑		'Emerging Buddha' ↕
2	2 AM ↑ 10 PM	II 'Knowledge of exiting and Re-appearing' (*cutūpapāta ñāṇa*) (REBIRTH)		"...according to their actions, bad .. leading to misery and good .. to a good destiny"		Samana Gotama
1	10 PM ↑ 6 PM	I 'Knowledge of former lives' (*pubbenivāsa-nānussati ñāṇa*) (REBIRTH)		"seeing how he himself was born in several life-times"		Samana Gotama

NOTES TO CHART

Column 3 shows how Knowledges I and II both relate to Rebirth /Re-becoming, and Knowledge III to end of both (Re)birth, which means also end of Death.

Column 5 shows how, in the first hour of Watch 3, knowledge of the framework of the Four Noble Truths – Suffering, Arising, Cessation and Path, emerges on the basis of the suffering come to be perceived in Watches 1 and 2, the upward arrow indicating this connection. The upward arrows in the Column also indicate that the interrelated details of each of the NT's come to be worked out as well, roughly one after the other, in the context of the framework.

'Emerging Buddha' in Column 7 against the 2 – 4 AM time slot of Watch 3 is not Canonical, but seeks to provide the bridge from Samana Gotama to Buddha.

The two-way arrow in Column 7 indicates that both attaining Nibbana and becoming Buddha takes place in the same process.

Likewise, the two-way arrow above it shows, again intuitively constructing, working through the details of the Path, based in the 'Bliss of Emancipation' (the texts allowing it a whole week out of the first seven weeks), includes reminiscing upon his newly experienced state of being, and double-checking for himself.

Works Cited

Alagiyawanna Mukaweti, c. 1600, Subhasitaya.

Analayo, 2003, Satipatthana, The Direct Path to Realization, Kandy: Buddhist Publication Society

Bachelor Stephen, 1977, Buddhism without Beliefs, Wisdom.

Bodmer, Walter & Robin McKie, 1994, The Book of Man: the Quest to Discover Our Genetic Heritage, Viking

Chalmers & Rouse (tr.), 1981, Jataka I & II , p. 197ff., London: Pali Text Society

Davids, Rhys and William Stede, 1979, Pali-English Dictionary, London: Pali Text Society

Digha Nikaya, Pali Text Society.

Frey-Rohn, Liliane, 974, From Freud to Jung: a Comparative Study of the Psychology of the Unconsciousness, Shambhala

Jayasuriya, W Γ, 1963, The Psychology and Philosophy of Buddhism, re-published: Motilal Banbarsidass

Kabat-Zinn, 1994; 2005, Wherever you go, there you are: mindfulness meditation in everyday life, NY: Hyperion

Kirkland, Glen & Richard Davies, 1996, Dimensions, Toronto: Gage.

Majjhima Nikaya, Pali Text Society.

McElvaine, Robert S, 2001, Eve's Seed: Biology, the Sexes and the Course of History, McGraw Hill

Morris, Richard, 1990, The Edges of Science: Crossing the boundary from physics to metaphysics, Prentice.

Nanamoli, Bhikkhu & Bhikkhu Bodhi, The Middle Length Discourses of the Buddha, 1995 / 2001, Wisdom.

Nyanaponika Thera & Hellmuth Hecker, 1997, Great Disciples of the Buddha, Wisdom

Nananada, Bhikkhu K (tr.), 2000 (of Vidagama Maitreya, Loweda Sangarawa, 16th C ACE) Towards a Better World, Sri Lanka: Department of Public Trustee, Dhamma Publications

Trust.

Reynolds, Christopher (ed.), 1970, An Anthology of Sinhalese Literature up to 1815, London: George Allen & Unwin, Unesco

Samyutta Nikaya, Pali Text Society.

Sugunasiri, Suwanda, 1990, "How non-Christians tackle abortion," Saturday Magazine, Toronto Star, Jan 6, M 19.

Sugunasiri, Suwanda H J, 1995, 'Whole Body, not Heart, as the Seat of Consciousness,' Phil. E & W, 45, 3.

------------------------, 2001, You're What you Sense: a Buddhianscientific Dialogue, Dehiwala: Buddhist Cultural Centre

------------------------, in preparation (2009), "'Asoulity,' not 'Selfless,' as best   capturing Buddha's concept of anattā."

Vidagama Maitreya, 15th c., Lowaeda Sangaraava (in Sinhala) 'A Treatise for the Good of the World.'

Warder, A K, 1970, Indian Buddhism, Motilal Banarsidass.

Webster's Dictionary.

Wilbur, Ken, Jack Engler and Daniel Brown, 1986, Transformations of Consciousness, New Science Library.

Endnotes

1   This piece has much to do with precision of language and meaning, and so it may be relevant to note that the author (linguist, writer and poet) has been featured for 'Precise thought and language in the essay' (see Kirkland & Davies, 1996).

2   Bachelor, 1977, p. 37 and 35 respectively.

3   The Pali term is paṭisotagāminipaṭipadā.

4   Upanishads are classical Hindu Religious works. See Sugunasiri, 1995 for the Buddha's view of the seat of consciousness.

5   It may be noted that 'ensoulment' is common to other theistic religions as well, such as e.g., Judaism, Christianity and Islam. See Sugunasiri, 1990, for a popular treatment.

6   The term is punabbhava. We may note with interest that the term punaruppatti, literally 're-birth,' does not occur in the Canon. However, jāti 'birth' does.

7   Davids and Stede, 1979.

8   I use the term 'Buddhian' to mean 'relating to the Buddha,' to be distinguished from 'Buddhist,' meaning 'having to do with cultural interpretations of Buddha's Teachings.'

9   See Sugunasiri (in preparation, 2009) for this translation of anattā.

10   You may sometimes read about 'gods' in Buddhism. This is very different from 'God,' with a capital G, i.e., creator god ('Brahman' in Hinduism). The gods (deva in Pali, meaning 'shining ones') of Buddhism are those who have been born into a happy state. They, too, however, are subject to change, and death, and depend on merit transferred by humans, following a meritorious deed such as offering alms to the Sangha (ordained men and women), paying homage to the Buddha, etc.

11   The confusion may stem from the fact that both Pali (re Buddhism) and Sanskrit (re Hinduism) come from the same etymological root, though used with different meanings. And if you're sharp, as I know you are, you'll note, and remember, the slightly different spelling (as following), and slightly different pronunciation as well. See if you can catch them:

PALI	SANSKRIT
punabbhava	punarbhava
punaruppatti	punarutpatti

We may also note here the Pali term punavàsa (S.I.200) (S = Samyutta Nikaya) is given in the Dictionary, with no Sanskrit cognate, meaning 'another existence.'

12 It is characterized as 'a light was born; an eye was born' (aloko udapādi cakkhum udapādi) (Ariyapariyesana Sutta, M.I. # 26 (M = Majjhima Nikaya)).

13 The Pali term for 'knowledge' is vijjā, and 'three knowledges' tevijjā, tisso vijjā or tayo vijjā.

14 Caturariya sacca.

15 1. Dukkha, 2. samudaya, 3. nirodha and 4. magga respectively.

16 Pubbenivāsanānussati ñāṇa < knowledge' (ñāṇa) ' [of] 'memory' (-anussati) [of his own] 'living' (-nivāsana-) 'in the past' (pubbe-). The lives recalled are collected in a book called Jātaka 'Birth Stories.' See Chalmers & Rouse, 1981.

17 About 50, as scholars now agree, the rest of the 500 Jātaka Birth Stories being clever, and sometimes unclever, tales, and fabrications, drawn upon folktales.

18 Maṇikaṇṭha Jātaka, # 253. See Chalmers & Rouse (tr.), 1981. Ananda was the Buddha's personal attendant during the last years of his life, and also called the 'Treasurer of the Dhamma' (dhamma bhāṇḍāgārika) for his extensive memory of the Buddha's Teachings.

19 The reference here is to Charles Darwin who is credited with the Theory of Evolution.

20 See Warder, 1970, 46 for the fuller text.

21 Nevasaññāñāsaññāyatana. Don't even ask me what that is. Let the diligent reach the shores by taking to the raft of meditation! All I can say is that it was a mind concentrated beyond measure, the mind-scientist, as I would like to characterize the Buddha, needling his way into subtler and subtler quarters of the mind.

22 Saññānirodha.

23 Ekaggatā.

24 This is the literal meanings of vijjā as in tevijjā (see Endnote 13).

25 How a stimulus, through one or more of the six senses (including the mind-sense), ends up as consciousness is well explained by the Buddha. See Jayasuriya, W F, 1963, for an academic treatment, and Sugunasiri, 2001, for a popular treatment.

26 "American Physicist Murray Gell-Mann and the Israeli physicist Yuval Ne'eman independently discovered that baryons and mesons could be grouped in sub-families in a particular natural way." The theory generated by the observations was "[c]hristened the Eightfold Way," drawn upon the Buddha's Noble Eightfold Path, "a pun ... because [the theory] put certain commonly observed mesons and baryons together in groups of eight." (Morris, 1990, p. 12). Later research finds the clustering to be of more than eight.

27 Davids & Stede, 1979.

28 In Pali, 'together' (sam-) + 'move along' (or flow) (-sāra < sarati). But behold! Sarati itself is from two roots. One is sṛ- with the meaning of 'to flow' (as above), but another is from smṛ- 'memory.' Behind the idea of rebirth/re-becoming would surely be memory (for otherwise there would be no continuity). So the term samsara seems to cleverly capture both ideas: (1) traveling together and (2) taking (some) memory with you into a next life. Neat-o!

29 Cutūpapatti < cuti + upapatti, on the basis of 'the breaking up of the body after dying' (kāyassa bhedā param maraṇā) (M.I, 23).

30 In Warder, 1970, p. 48.

31 Tabula rasa is a concept introduced by John Locke, British philosopher, to characterize the nature of the mind of a human infant at birth – blank, with nothing in it. This 17th c. view has now been shown to be wrong, and patriarchal. See McElvaine, 2001: 222 for a critique, and for other references to Locke.

32 "I posit the world in this two fathom body," declares the Buddha. What this means is that a given individual's world is only what s/he comes to experience through her/his senses, and nothing more. For example, had you not encountered this article, it would not be part of your world, any more than you, the reader, to me, having never encountered you. For details, see Sugunasiri, 2001.

33 Those of a scientific bent, who look to go beyond the Webster meaning of empirical as observation and experiment, may be looking for other criteria such as 'repeatability' and 'cross validity.' Can Samana Gotama's experiment be repeated by others? Could the findings be validated through comparison? For sure. In fact, there are disciples, ten male and ten female, who Buddha himself recognizes to have achieved the same levels of meditational sophistication as his own (see Nyanaponika & Hecker,1997, for a study). Perhaps there could be some in our own time, too. But would we ever know? Nope. Because Buddha puts a damper on putting one's spiritual linen on public display.

However, the sophistication reached by the disciples, bringing the same results points to the fact that only those who have trained themselves in meditation can establish cross-validity and repeatability. This is no more than saying that only trained scientists can personally verify Einstein's theories.

Regarding cross-validity and repeatability, we may also refer readers to early studies by Wilbur, Engler and Brown (1986). You may want to update yourself on a more recent studies.

34 Paṭisandhi citta = upapatti (see also Endnote. 29).

35 It is interesting that science is full of such moments of creative genius. We have the well

known example of Archimedes, a 3rd c. BCE, mathematician and physicist, assigned the task of determining whether the gold in the King's crown was what the craftsman said it was, i.e., genuine gold. Mulling over this, one day he steps into a filled-to-the-brim bathtub, and voila, the answer comes to him. The genuineness or otherwise of the crown could be determined by placing it in a container filled to the brim with water, and then measuring the volume of water displaced. This would help determine the volume of the crown. Then by weighing the crown, its weight could be determined. By dividing the weight by the volume, the specific gravity of the crown can be established, telling the scientist whether the crown is pure gold or an alloy, i.e., a mixture with another metal, like copper.

Another example comes from the 19th c. French mathematician, Jules-Henri Poincaré: "In a famous essay titled Mathematical Creation, [he] recalled an aha moment involving a particular kind of mathematical construct known as 'Fuchsian functions.' For two weeks he struggled to prove a particular property of these functions, but writes that he 'tried a great number of combinations and reached no results.' A few days later he left his home in Caen, France, to join some colleagues on a geological excursion to Coutances, where he recalls boarding an omnibus. 'At the moment when I put my foot on the step the idea came to me, without anything in my former thoughts seeming to have paved the way for it,' he wrote. 'On my return to Caen, for conscience's sake I verified the result at my leisure.' Poincaré was not yet 30." (I am thankful for Prof. Helmut Burkhardt of Ryerson University for the details.)

You may want to see if you have in your experience examples of spontaneity – that is something popping up to your mind when you're not thinking about it.

36   The line continues: "... ageing ...., dying..., grief..., lamentation..., pain...., depression... misery..., not getting what one   wants is suffering." (Saccavibhanga sutta, M III, 141.)

37   Taṇhā.

38   The term for both human and animal is sattā.

39   See Sugunasiri, 2001, for a discussion.

40   Sabbe sattā āhāraṭṭhitikā.

41   "Freud built the psychology of the unconscious essentially on the basis of instinctual factors....: Drive impulse, craving, tension of needs..." This 'vital drive' he calls 'eros' (Frey-Rohn, 1974, p. 104).

42   Thanatos is from Greek mythology, although Freud who "opposed the vital drive (eros) to the death drive," also speaks of a similar instinct (op.cit.).

43   Kāma taṇhā, bhava taṇhā, vibhava taṇhā.

44   Katamo cÆāvuso dukkhasamudayo? YāÆyam tanhā ponobhavikā... (M.I.48)

45   Rāga, dosa, moha.

46 See Nanananda (tr.), 2000, verse # 40.

47 Ayam antimā jāti; natthidāni punabbhavo.

48 Ajāta.

49 Amata.

50 Khīnāsava.

51 Khīnā jāti (D.I.84) (D = Digha Nikaya).

52 Ariyapariyesana Sutta, M.I., 26.

53 Mahākāruṇiko, it being in balance with paññā ' wisdom' .

54 So what is this Path? It is called the Noble Eightfold Path, because it is made up of eight steps. In its ideal (= 'Noble') form, each is characterized as being 'Excellent': Excellent View; Excellent Conceptualization; Excellent Language; Excellent Conduct; Excellent Livelihood; Excellent Exercise; Excellent Mindfulness and Excellent Concentration. See Warder, op. cit., 100-105 for a brief treatment.

55 Kamma we understand here as 'action' and 'consequence.'

56 The break-up of this Third watch into 4 segments is my own attempt to understand the process, and is not Canonical. By the beginning of the Third Watch, he would already have come by the first Truth of Suffering, based in the first two Watches. So I would guess that the first hour or so of this Third Watch (2 to 3) went by trying to figure out the cause of suffering (Second Truth), and 3 to 4 in arriving at an understanding of the Third Truth, i.e., the solution as being the ditching of cankers, and doing the ditching itself in the process. So now we are into the 4 to 5 AM time slot when he would be figuring out the Fourth Truth. The final hour may be seen as reckoning time – bringing to mind the overall experience if only to see he's got it right, and that he was not mistaken or deluded. This would be like a scientist or a researcher checking things out again, after arriving at some results, just to make sure.

57 'Double helix' refers to the two strands of a gene that divides, but each growing into another gene again with two strands. See Bodmer & McKie, 1994, 42 ff for a discussion.

58 Āsavakkhaya ñāṇa.

59 Buddha characterizes his Teaching as an ehi passika 'come and see.'

60 Vibhajjavādin, as the Buddha is seen, at least in the Theravada tradition.

61 Ucchedavāda and -āśvatavāda respectively. Brahmajala sutta, D.1.

62 With well-sharpened minds of their own, cultivated in meditation, Brahmin practitioners may have been able to see what the Buddha himself saw. Alternatively, rebirth may have developed as a speculative concept well fitting a niche called for by their understanding of 're-incarnation' with the hand of God at work.

63 This is not to say that everything has been proven either. Historically, it has taken western

science over two thousand years before discovering the validity of some of Buddha's discoveries. Mindfulness Meditation leaps to one's mind as perhaps the most recent high profile example (see, e.g., studies by Kabat-Zinn, 1994, 2005). And so it should not be surprising that it may yet be a while before western science gets the technological sophist-cation to come by the validity of Rebirth as reality.

64   Majjhima Nikaya, 10. See Nanamoli & Bodhi, 1995 / 2001, 145 ff.

65   See Analayo, 2003, for an in-depth treatment.

66   Aetat naetat paralova sudaneni mahata
Halot yeheki pavkam no tabama sita.
(Alagiyawanna Mukaweti, Subhasitaya 'The Well-Spoken' (c.1600). See also Reynolds (ed.), 1970, for another selection from Alagiyawanna.)

(Please send your comments to *suwanda.sugunasiri@utoronto.ca*)

About the Author

US Fulbright Scholar Suwanda H. J. Sugunasiri is Founding Editor of the Canadian Journal of Buddhist Studies (*http://jps.library.utoronto.ca/index.php/cjbs/*), and is the author of You are What You Sense: a BuddhianScientific Dialogue and Embryo as Person: Buddhism, Bioethics and Society. His seminal paper, "The Whole Body, not Heart, as 'Seat of Consciousness': the Buddha's View" (Philosophy East and West, 45.3) challenges the traditional view. Founder of Nalanda College of Buddhist Studies, Toronto, Canada, and Adjunct Professor, Faculty of Divinity, Trinity College, University of Toronto, he is also Editor of Thus Spake the Sangha, presenting the life stories of five Sangha Elders of Toronto. Columnist in the Toronto Star from a Buddhist perspective, he is Past President of the Buddhist Council of Canada.

About Sumeru

The Sumeru Press Inc. is a Canadian publisher of Buddhist books and art. Sumeru also maintains a blog on Canadian Buddhism and offers publishing consulting services to Buddhist organizations and initiatives.

Recent Sumeru projects include a redesign of the Buddhism in Canada website (*www.buddhismcanada.com*) last year. Earlier this year, Sumeru completed a year-long research and development project for the University of Toronto and the Buddhist Education Foundation for Canada, the goal of which was to lay the groundwork for an online scholarly journal dealing with Buddhism and Psychology.

For more information about Sumeru and Canadian Buddhism, please visit *www.sumeru-books.com* or *www.sumeru.ca*